SPECTRUM®
READERS

LEVEL 1

P9-CQH-712

LOOK!
Nature's Helpers

By Katharine Kenah

 Carson-Dellosa
Publishing

SPECTRUM®

An imprint of Carson-Dellosa Publishing, LLC
P.O. Box 35665
Greensboro, NC 27425-5665

carsondellosa.com

Printed in the USA. All rights reserved.
ISBN 978-1-62399-135-7

01-002131120

Some living things
work in pairs.
They help each other.
They are nature's
amazing partners.

Clown Fish and Sea Anemone

What do they do?
The clown fish cleans
the sea anemone.
The sea anemone keeps
the clown fish safe.

Tickbird and Rhinoceros

What do they do?
The tickbird keeps the
rhinoceros free of bugs.
The rhinoceros keeps the
tickbird full of food.

Elephant and Egret

What do they do?
The elephant kicks
bugs into the air.
The egret eats the bugs.

Pitcher Plant and Tree Frog

What do they do?
The pitcher plant draws
in bugs with its colors.
The tree frog eats the bugs.

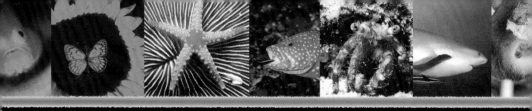

Plover and Crocodile

What do they do?
The plover cleans out food
from the crocodile's teeth.
The crocodile gives the plover
food to eat.

Oxpecker and Antelope

What do they do?
The oxpecker eats bugs
from the antelope's back.
The antelope gives the
oxpecker food to eat.

Flower and Hummingbird

What do they do?
The flower has food
for the hummingbird.
The hummingbird helps
more flowers to grow.

Goby and Sea Urchin

What do they do?
The goby helps the
sea urchin find food.
The sea urchin helps
the goby stay safe.

Sunflower and Butterfly

What do they do?
The sunflower has
food for the butterfly.
The butterfly helps more
sunflowers to grow.

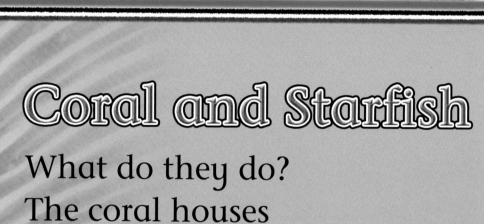

Coral and Starfish

What do they do?
The coral houses
many small animals.
The starfish eats
these animals.

Wrasse and Grouper

What do they do?
The wrasse cleans bugs
from the grouper.
The grouper gives the
wrasse food to eat.

Hermit Crab and Sea Anemone

What do they do?
The hermit crab helps the
sea anemone find food.
The sea anemone makes
the hermit crab hard to see.

Shark and Remora

What do they do?
The shark gives the
remora a free ride.
The remora eats the food
that the shark does not.

Algae and Sloth

What do they do?
The sloth uses the green
algae to hide in a tree.
The algae grows well
in the sloth's fur.

LOOK! Nature's Helpers
Comprehension Questions

1. What does it mean for animals to work in pairs?

2. How does a clown fish help a sea anemone?

3. Why do you think the tickbird needs the rhinoceros?

4. How does the elephant help the egret?

5. How does a pitcher plant draw in bugs?

6. Why do you think the crocodile needs the plover?

7. What do you think would happen if the antelope did not have the oxpecker as a partner?

8. How does the butterfly help the sunflower?

9. What is a wrasse?